RHINOC
LEARN ABOUT THE RHINO

BEAUTIFUL PHOTOS & AMAZING ANIMAL FUN FACTS

REAL ANIMAL PHOTOS WITH INTERESTING FUN FACTS

SELENA DALE
www.selenadale.com

COPYRIGHT NOTICE

Copyright© 2018 by Selena Dale

All Rights Reserved.

©SELENA DALE
Copyright 2018

All rights reserved. No part of this publication may be reproduced, stored in retrieval system, copied in any form or by any means, electronic, mechanical, photocopying, recording or otherwise transmitted without written permission from the publisher. Please do not participate in or encourage piracy of this material in any way. You must not circulate this book in any format. SELENA DALE does not control or direct users' actions and is not responsible for the information or content shared, harm and/or actions of the book readers.

In accordance with the U.S. Copyright Act of 1976, the scanning, uploading and electronic sharing of any part of this book without the permission of the publisher constitute unlawful piracy and theft of the author's intellectual property.

Thank you for your support of the author's rights.

CONTENTS

INTRODUCTION 1
LET'S LEARN ABOUT RHINOS 3
MORE BESTSELLING KIDS BOOKS 20
REQUESTING A FAVOR… 22

INTRODUCTION

Welcome to another edition of the "Learn About" book series. In this book you will learn lots of fun and interesting facts about an amazing animal called a Rhinoceros.

There are full color photos on every page...sometimes two per page! You and your child can have fun looking at these fascinating images while learning and understanding the world of animals.

This book focuses on younger readers who still need that visual content to help them understand what they are reading.

The "Learn About" book series is suited to 3 year olds and upwards and is perfect for parent or guardian to read with the child.

The book has a simple layout so your child can follow along while reading or being read to.

The information is concise and filled with as much learning information as possible while keeping the content fun and relaxing for all to read.

LET'S LEARN ABOUT RHINOS

The rhinoceros gets its name from a word meaning "nose horn" because all species of rhinos have either one or two horns on their nose.

There are five different species of rhinoceros in the world. Two of them are native to Africa and three live in Southeast Asia.

The two African rhinoceros species are among the five heaviest land mammals in the world. Male rhinos can reach weights of five thousand pounds or 2,300 kilograms. That is a very heavy animal!

Rhinos are really big animals because even the Sumatran rhinoceros, which is the smallest species, reaches lengths of eight feet or 2.5 meters!

SUMATRAN RHINOCEROS

The white rhino, which is the largest of all rhinoceroses, may grow as long as 13 feet or 4 meters. They are the biggest of these "nose horn" animals but they have very little hair on their bodies. Most of their hair is on their ears and the tip of their tail.

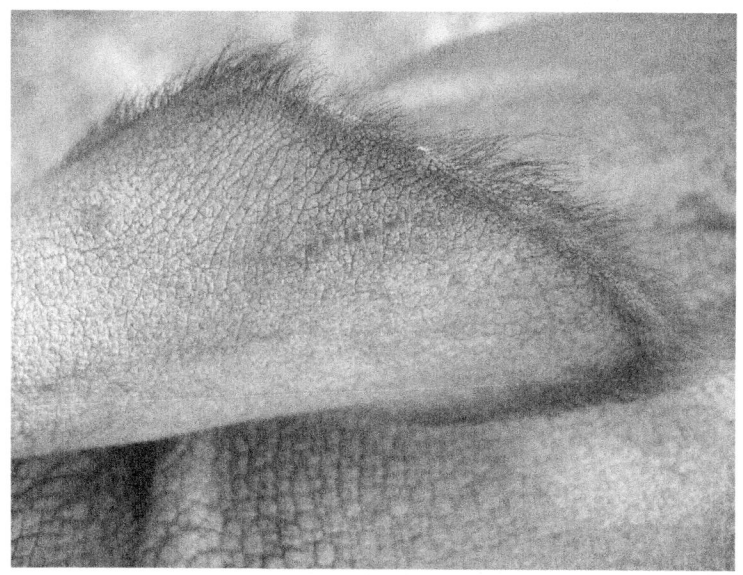

RHINOCEROS EAR

All rhinoceroses are mammals which means they are warm-blooded, they need to breathe air and they feed their babies with milk.

Rhinos are herbivores which means they eat mostly vegetation such as leaves from trees and bushes. Some types of rhinoceros eat mostly grass.

Rhinos have thick greyish skin which wrinkles and folds like plates of armor.

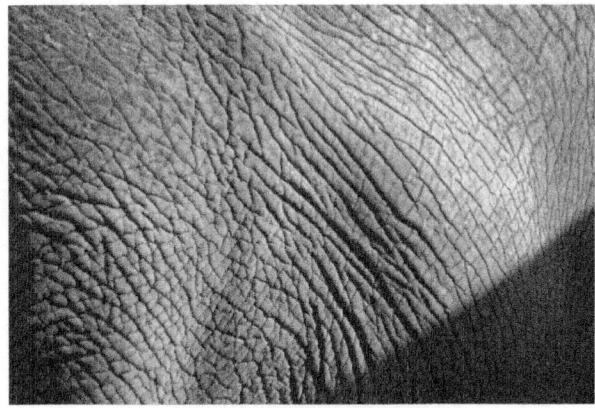

RHINOCEROS SKIN

Although their skin is thick and strong it is not enough to protect them from the Sun and biting insects. Rhinos have a special way of avoiding those pesky mosquitoes...they use mud.

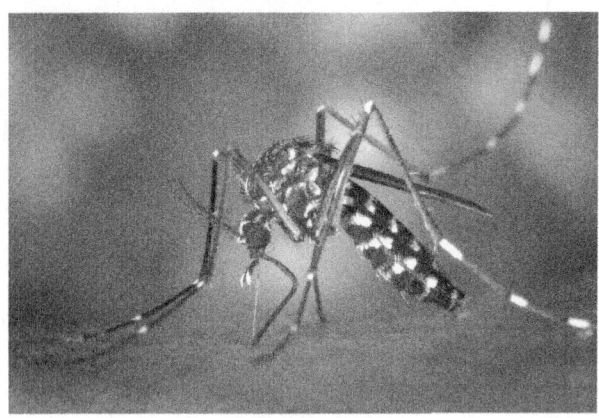

MOSQUITO

RHINO PLAYING IN MUD

RHINOS ENJOYING A MUD BATH

Rhinoceroses love to wallow in mud. The more mud they can cover themselves with the better. Thick layers of mud act like a natural sunblock preventing sunburns and make it difficult for insects to bite their skin.

Wallowing in the mud also helps rhinos to cool off on hot days meaning that a muddy rhino is a happy rhino.

Rhino rhinoceros have three toes on each foot and each toe ends with a blunt toenail.

They have poor eyesight but keen hearing and an excellent sense of smell which they rely on to help them find food and identify threats in general.

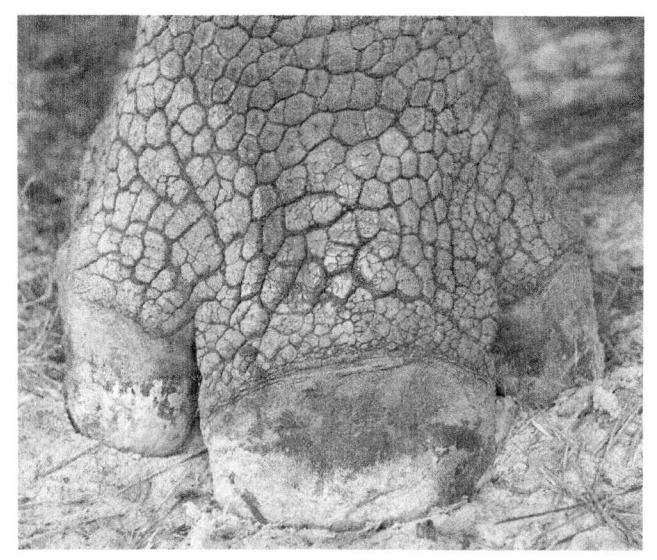

RHINOCEROS FOOT

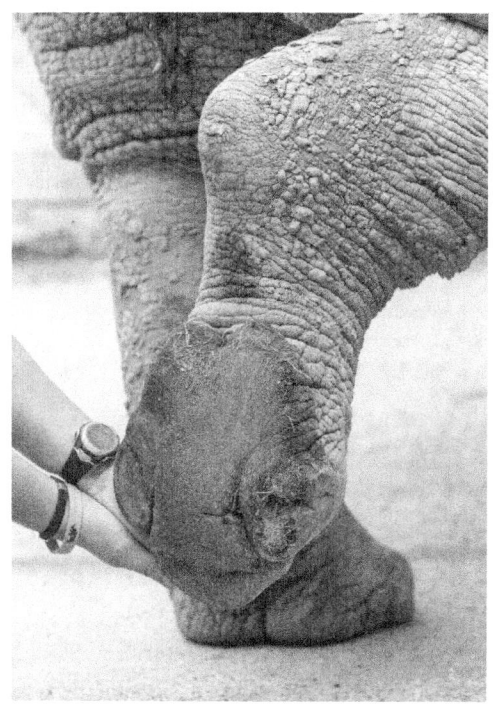

RHINOCEROS EYS & NOSE

Rhinos are solitary animals and prefer to live alone but some species of rhinoceros will live in groups of up to ten members.

MOMMY RHINO AND HER BABY

A male rhinoceros is called a bull, a female id called a cow and the young are called a calves. A group of rhinos is called a "crash".

A CRASH OF RHINOCEROSES

Rhinoceroses usually avoid contact with people but aggressive males or mothers with calves may charge without much any warning.

Despite their large size rhinoceros can charge at speeds of up to 30 miles per hour or 45 km/h. That is pretty fast for such a heavy animal.

Although an adult rhinoceros has no natural predators rhinoceroses are some of the most endangered species on earth. They are killed by humans for their horns. This is not good news!

RHINOCEROS HORNS

Rhino horns are made of keratin, the same material that makes our hair and fingernails but some people believe that they can be used as medicine.

People are willing to pay a lot of money for rhinoceros horns which is why bad people called poachers are killing these beautiful animals.

RESTING RHINOS

SOME RHINOS EAT GRASS

The poachers are killing so many rhinos that some species are at the brink of extinction!

There is some good news though!

People all over the world are working hard to try to save the rhinoceros. These big heavy animals are very well looked after in places called, wildlife reserves. These good people are doing their best to guard rhinos from poachers.

Rhinos are happy in wildlife reserves because they are free to roam the land without being in any danger from poachers.

The people who run the reserves are very dedicated and do their very best to keep all rhinoceroses safe and healthy.

HAPPY RHINOS IN A WILDLIFE RESERVE

MORE BESTSELLING KIDS BOOKS AT:-

www.selenadale.com

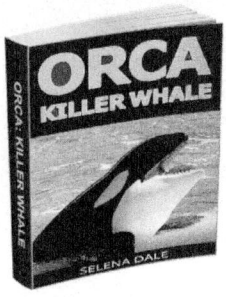  

REQUESTING A FAVOR...

Dear Valued Customer,

Selena Dale does her best to create quality books for children and without your support she would not be able to do so.

Therefore, if you enjoyed this book, **PLEASE spare a few moments to leave a review on this book's Amazon product page.**

Each and every one of your reviews would be greatly appreciated.

Selena is forever grateful for your support...**THANK YOU!**

Sincerely,
Selena Dale
www.selenadale.com

Printed in Great Britain
by Amazon